# ABRACADABRA

**Tap Your Way to Happiness**

**With Gran and Jimby**

Publisher:  Raewyn Weller Enterprises New Zealand

First published:  October 2021

Author:  Raewyn Weller (NZ)

Cover and content Illustrated by M. Ridho Mentarie

ISBN 978-0-473-59765-8

The information within has been produced as general

guidance to empower readers in their search

to be happy and healthy

Emotionally, Physically, and Mentally.

It is not intended as medical advice.

The Author is happy for the material within to be used for

educational purposes in schools and organisations.

This book is dedicated to all the children in the world.

Especially my beautiful Children,

Grand and Great Grandchildren

Stephen, Louise and Julie

Elesha, Courtney, Jeremy, Eden and Kaitlyn

Lucah, Braxton, Summer, Mia, Isla, Keone

and those yet to arrive

Thank you to my family, clients and friends
for the suggestions, encouragement and support.

**Every Child is SPECIAL and deserves to be happy**

Hi Kids, I am Gran nice to meet you. When I was a kid, I always wanted to have a pet monkey, but in New Zealand we can't have pet monkeys, they are only in the zoo.
So when I grew up, I bought myself a monkey, his name is Jimby and he makes me happy.

I have learnt a fun way to feel better about myself when I am not feeling so good.  So together Jimby and I are going to have lots of fun teaching you how you can make yourself happier when you are feeling hurt, angry, worried or sad.

Hey Kids, I'm Jimby. I am looking forward to showing you all how to change how you feel when you are unhappy, scared, worried or angry.

ABRACADABRA - You are a magician!
Did you know that you can change how you think, feel and act?
You CAN do it, you can make yourself feel happier.

Would you like to learn how?

Yes Please

Did you know that we all have emotions? Sometimes we feel sad, scared, angry, worried, ashamed, guilty, unloved, or not good enough.
Other times we feel happy, we feel loved, proud, clever, strong and brave. These are all emotions.
It is great to feel happy emotions, but sometimes we feel unhappy and hurting inside. It is ok to to feel unhappy for a short time every now and then, we all feel these emotions at times.
But it is not so good to feel like that most of the time.
If you are hurting, sad or angry most of the time it affects your health, and you can get sick easily.
Let's see what some emotions that we feel might look like.
I am putting on a happy face. Gran can you show what proud looks like?
Now it's your turn, can you to show us different emotions  that you feel?

Jimby is so excited that Gran is letting him teach the kids how to change how they feel when they are feeling sad or have unwanted emotions.
"We start off with doing the Karate Chop," says Jimby
You tap on the side of one hand below your little finger with the fingers on your other hand, like this. The kids all practice doing the Karate Chop.

Well done, it's easy and fun isn't it?
Yep sure is the kids shout out.
Jimby carries on, "we always start with the Karate Chop, it is the first of ten happy points you are going to learn. They are all energy points on our body that have been used for hundreds of years, by thousands of people to help them feel better.  Cool aye."

"Real cool" says Charlie, "please show us how. We want to be happy and learn about our emotions and the ways you can help us."

Ok, lets go then. As we do the Karate Chop we say how we are feeling, then we say we love ourself and we are still a cool kid.

For example, I wet my bed. Oops! don't tell anyone.
I would say: Even though I wet my bed and I feel embarrassed,
I love myself anyway and I am a cool kid.
I say that 3 times while doing the Karate Chop.
Let's try it together.

Tama says "but I don't wet my bed!"
So tell me what makes you feel sad, upset or hurt Tama?
My mum and dad always growl me and I don't always know why. It makes me angry and I throw things around.

Thanks for sharing Tama, you can practice karate chopping that away, say those words.
Now each of you can quietly say what is upsetting you as you do the Karate Chop.
Say whatever you are sad, upset, worried or hurting about.
Tell the real truth about how you are feeling, as this lets it out so you can feel better and happier.

Jimby is excited to be teaching the kids! Let's go kids, start doing the Karate Chop. Remember we say what our problem is 3 times.
I say "Even though I wet my bed and I feel embarrassed about it, I love myself anyway, I am still a cool kid."
You say, "Even though I… (say whatever you are sad or worried about), I love myself anyway, I am a cool kid."

They all practice the Karate Chop while saying what is upsetting them.

"You are all doing so well," says Gran.
Jimby can you please show the kids what comes next.

Sure Gran, learning really is a game.
We have 9 more points that we tap with the tips of our fingers, about 7 times
on each point as we say how we are really feeling.
I will show you where the points are.
In the middle of top of your head, is your **Thinking point**
On the insides of your eyebrows is your **Seeing point**
On your temples, at the outside of your eyes is your **Listening point**
Under your eyes on your cheek bones is your **Smiling point**
Under your nose is your **Smelling point**
Under your lips, on your chin is your **Tasting point**
Just below your collar bone, where Tarzan hits on his chest, is your **Brave point**
Under your arms is your **Hugging point** and
**Clapping wrists is your last point**

Jimby laughs, "look at the rabbit he wants to learn too, he's starting with the tasting point. Ok kids let's practice, say the name of each point out loud as we tap them together."

Here we go:

Karate Chop
Thinking point
Seeing point
Listening point
Smiling point
Smelling point
Tasting point
Brave point
Hugging point
Clapping wrists

"Wow you are all doing so well," says Gran. Before you start I want you all to close your eyes, take a BIG breath in and hold onto it.
Now I want you to think how bad you feel about whatever you are sad, angry, hurting or worried about.
From 1 – 10, 1 is not bad, and 10 is really bad. What number do you feel?
Jimby shared that he was so embarrassed about wetting the bed his number is 8.
The kids were all keen to share and called out what they were feeling.
Tama said 'mine is 7,' Charlie '9,' Kathy 'mine is 8,' Sameer '6,' and Hannah said '7.'
"Thank you for sharing," says Gran, "remember that number for later."

Can anyone tell me if they can feel that feeling in their body?
Close your eyes again, take a big breath in and see if you can feel the sadness, anger or worry anywhere in your body.
If so, would you like to share with us where in your body you are feeling it? Is it in your Heart? Your Head? Your Throat?

"It's in my tummy," says Charlie. Tama says "I feel it in my heart," Hannah points to her head and Sameer puts his hand on his heart. Kathy says sadly, "I can't feel anything."

Its ok if you can't feel anything like Kathy, we can't always feel it.
"Thank you for sharing, with me and Jimby," says Gran.

Jimby is really excited now!
I am so proud of you.
Let's do it from the start with the Karate Chop saying whatever is troubling you.
Remember say it 3 times just like before.

Even though the kids
at school are mean
to me and I get upset
I love myself anyway,
I am a cool kid

Even though I feel
scared when I get
asthma
I love myself,
I am an ok kid

Even though
mum and dad
always growl me
and I get mad,
I love myself anyway,
I am a ka pai kid

Even though
my dad left us and
I think it's my fault,
I love myself anyway,
I am a cool kid

Even though
I find it hard to learn
I love myself anyway,
I am a lovely girl

Gran laughs! even our rabbit and bird friends are joining in.
Smiling Jimby says, "ok now onto the other points, just follow
Gran and me." "Let's do it together, starting at the top of your head
with your Thinking point."
"Tap each point about 7 times as you say how you are really feeling.
As you move to the next point you say something else you are feeling.
We go through all the 9 points 3 times round.
After clapping your wrists go back up
to the top of your head."

"Our rabbit and bird friends are really enjoying tapping," says Gran,
"they must need help too."
Now back up to the top and continue to tap saying the different things you
are feeling until you have tapped the 9 points 2 more times.
I feel hurt
Everyone says I am a baby
Mum gets mad at me
They laugh at me
Dad doesn't love me
I feel dumb
I feel silly

Jimby is feeling so good, he tells them all to stand up and take a stretch.
Now take a big breath in and really feel inside you.
Feel how you are feeling, what number from 1 to 10 are you at now?

"Wow learning really is a game and you are all doing so well,"
says Gran. "I feel much better too. It's fun isn't it!"
Can you see how it has made you all feel much better?
The kids all smile in agreement, all eager to share their number as they are
all feeling so much better. They all want to keep learning.

Next we move on to say how we are feeling now.
Just like before, go back to the Karate Chop, but this time you say
how you are feeling now, knowing that you are feeling better.
Imagine all your sadness, anger, worries or hurt has gone or is going.
You can say;
Even though I still feel a little sad, I am feeling happier, and I love myself,
I am a cool kid.
Or even though I still feel a little angry, it's getting better, I love myself,
I am a great kid.
Or even though I might still feel a little unhappy, I love myself anyway,
I am a cool kid.
Can anyone tell me how many times do we do the Karate Chop?

Jimby starts off, "I feel ok now, I'm staying dry at night, I love myself and I am a cool monkey."
The kids smile, imagining and saying their changes as they do the karate chop.

I am so proud of you all.
Gran please join in again as we tap the other points.
Remember tap each point 7 times as you say what emotions you are feeling now, and go 3 times around all 9 points.
They all start tapping at their Thinking Point, saying how they are feeling.
Jimby stands watching and smiling, feeling proud of them, as he reminds them what to do.
I feel happy, everyone thinks I am cool
Life is ka pai, mum and dad are nice to me
I feel loved, Life is fun
I feel good about myself, I am breathing much better
I am so happy with myself, I feel so proud

Wow you are doing so good, you can sit down again.

Now I want you to take a big breath in, hold it and feel how you feel now.
What number from 1 to 10 are you at now?

Thank you so much everyone for sharing and thank you Jimby for being such a great teacher.
"It's so much fun learning tapping isn't it!" says Jimby.
"Can you see how it has made you all feel much better?"
The rabbit and birds have even brought their friends to learn.
I feel so good now, I am happy, I think mum and dad will be too
Even the rabbits and birds are happy
It sure made me feel better
Can we do it again I feel much happier, and it was fun?
I want to show my friends to help them

Gran replied to Hannah saying, if you need to you can do it over and over until you will feel better and better.
Learning and teaching is a game said Jimby, how about you all teach your mums and dads, and maybe your teachers.
I am sure they get sad, worried, angry or hurt at times.

The kids all laugh!
It sure has been fun
They sure do need it

Emotional Freedom Tapping seems a little like magic.
But there is nothing magic about it.
It works for children and adults.
When you tap on your body's energy points,
your energy changes, when your energy
changes, your life changes.
Changing your thoughts, feelings, and emotions
shift your mind and body to an improved
healthier state.
Tapping uses ancient Chinese acupressure techniques along with modern world psychology. Together they help relieve stress, anxiety and pain. It can even help you sleep better.

You can use tapping on anything that makes you unhappy, sad,
angry, worried, or hurting in any way.
It will shift your energy to a much healthier
And happier emotional, mental and
physical state.
Always remember that the words you say
and the pictures you create in your mind
create your life.

Aroha 
Gran and Jimby